POPCORN treats

Fresh Popped Fun!

Popcorn Equivalents

1 (3 oz.) bag of microwave popcorn can yield anywhere from 6 to 10 cups of popped corn, depending on brand and the microwave used for popping

½ cup of popcorn kernels yields about 12 cups of popped corn *(the type and brand of kernels – as well as popping method – all have an effect on quantity)*

For the sake of your teeth, always remove any unpopped kernels after popping.

Printed in the United States of America
by G&R Publishing Co.

Distributed By:

Products

507 Industrial Street
Waverly, IA 50677

ISBN 978-1-56383-525-4
Item #7114

Ready to pop?

Unless specifically stated in a recipe, you can use purchased popcorn or make it yourself. It's easy!

Popped on the stovetop

Simply put enough vegetable oil or popcorn oil in a heavy saucepan to cover the bottom and add a few popcorn kernels to test the heat; cover the pan and place over medium heat. When those kernels pop, your oil is hot. Carefully add ½ C. of kernels *(to make 12 C.)*, cover, and cook until the popping nearly stops, shaking the pan constantly. Remove the pan from the heat and set aside until the popping stops completely or you'll have *crazy popcorn* flying everywhere!

Popped in a popper

Follow manufacturer's instructions.

Microwave popcorn

Follow package directions.

DIY microwave popcorn

Mix ¼ cup popcorn kernels and ½ teaspoon canola oil in a medium microwave-safe bowl. Cover with a microwave-safe plate and microwave on high 3 to 4 minutes or until there are 3 to 4 seconds between pops. Remove the bowl and plate using oven mitts.

Popcorn Angel Cake

Ingredients

- 2 (3 oz.) bags buttered microwave popcorn
- 1 (10.5 oz.) pkg. Reese's Pieces
- ¾ C. dry roasted peanuts
- ¾ C. candy corn
- ½ C. butter
- 1 (16 oz.) bag mini marshmallows

Get Started

Generously grease a large angel food tube pan with cooking spray. Pop the popcorn as directed on the package and transfer it to a large bowl; remove unpopped kernels. Add the Reese's Pieces, peanuts, and candy corn; toss well and set aside.

In a big greased microwave-safe bowl, microwave the butter just until melted. Add the marshmallows and microwave on high for 1½ to 2 minutes; stir until melted and smooth. Pour over the popcorn mixture and stir until well combined and coated. Press mixture into the prepared pan. Cover with foil and let cool at least 1 hour.

Run a knife around the edge of the pan to loosen the cake. To remove the cake, flip the pan over onto a large plate. Slice with a serrated knife. Serves 18

1 Cheesy Taco

Preheat oven to 300°. In a big bowl, combine 1 (3 oz.) bag buttered microwave popcorn, 2 C. pretzels, 2 C. cheddar-flavored Goldfish crackers, and 1 C. unsalted dry roasted peanuts. Mix ⅓ C. melted butter, ⅓ C. hot sauce, and 2 T. taco seasoning; pour over the popcorn mixture, stirring to coat well. Spread out on a parchment paper-lined baking sheet and bake for 40 minutes, stirring several times; cool. **Makes 9 cups**

2 Everything Bagel

Put 12 C. popcorn and 4 C. broken roasted garlic-flavored bagel chips in a big bowl. Stir together 6 T. melted butter, 2 T. sesame seed, 1 T. each caraway seed and dried minced onion, and ¾ tsp. each dried minced garlic and coarse salt. Pour seasoned butter over the popcorn mixture and stir to blend. **Makes 16 cups**

3 Parm & Pepper

Put 16 C. popcorn in a big bowl. Stir together ½ C. shredded Parmesan cheese and 1 tsp. each coarse black pepper and salt. In a separate small bowl, mix 3 T. melted butter and 1 T. olive oil; drizzle over the popcorn and stir until well coated. Sprinkle the cheese mixture over the top and stir until well blended. **Makes 16 cups**

4 Garlic-Basil

In a big bowl, combine 10 C. buttered popcorn, 1 C. Corn Chex cereal, and ½ C. golden raisins. Heat 3 T. olive oil in a skillet over medium heat. Stir in 2 tsp. dried basil and ½ tsp. each garlic powder and red pepper flakes; cook for 1 minute, stirring constantly. Add 1½ C. almonds and cook 3 minutes longer, stirring constantly. Add to bowl with popcorn; toss to blend. Sprinkle with some Parmesan cheese and toss again. **Makes 11 cups**

Butter Toffee Popcorn

Ingredients

4 (3 oz.) bags. salted microwave popcorn (unbuttered)

2 C. salted dry roasted peanuts

1 C. butter

2 ¼ C. brown sugar

¾ C. dark corn syrup

½ tsp. salt

1 tsp. baking soda

2 tsp. vanilla

Get Started

Preheat the oven to 250° and line two rimmed baking sheets with parchment paper. Pop the popcorn according to package directions, remove unpopped kernels, and dump into a big bowl along with the peanuts; set aside.

Melt the butter in a saucepan over medium heat. Add brown sugar, syrup, and salt, stirring constantly until it begins to boil. Boil for 3 minutes, stirring constantly. Remove from the heat and stir in the baking soda and vanilla *(it will get foamy)*. Pour over the popcorn and stir to coat. Spread onto the prepared baking sheets and bake for 1 hour, stirring every 15 minutes. Let cool 10 minutes before breaking apart. **Makes about 26 cups**

To make Butter Toffee-Coated Apples, wash and dry your favorite apples and insert sticks. Line a tray with waxed paper; butter the paper. Follow the directions on a bag of caramels to make caramel apples. While caramel is still wet, pack Butter Toffee Popcorn around each apple and set on prepared tray. *(This recipe will cover about 25 apples.)*

Thai Chicken Bites

Ingredients

1½ lbs. boneless skinless
  chicken breasts

1 egg

1 tsp. soy sauce

½ tsp. minced garlic

½ tsp. hot pepper sauce,
  or more to taste

2 C. popcorn

½ C. peanuts

Vegetable oil

Get Started

Cut the chicken into bite-size pieces. In a medium bowl, whisk together the egg, soy sauce, garlic, and hot sauce. Add chicken pieces and toss until well coated. Cover and let marinate about 10 minutes.

Meanwhile, process the popcorn in a blender or food processor until finely ground *(you should have about 1½ cups)*. Grind up the peanuts in the same way. Mix popcorn and peanuts in a shallow dish and set aside.

Preheat the oven to 350°. Remove the chicken from the marinade and coat each piece with the popcorn mixture. Heat 3 tablespoons oil in a large oven-proof skillet over medium-high heat. Place the chicken in the skillet and brown pieces on all sides, reducing the heat to medium and adding more oil as needed for even browning. Transfer the skillet to the oven and bake 12 to 15 minutes or until cooked through. Serve with Thai peanut sauce or sweet and sour sauce.

Makes about 40

Sweet & Salty Sticks

Ingredients

16 caramels

2 tsp. water

6 large pretzel rods

6 C. salted popcorn

1 square chocolate
almond bark

Decorating sprinkles

Heat the caramels and water in a double boiler until melted, stirring occasionally *(you can do this in the microwave instead, but you will need to reheat periodically to keep the caramel warm and spreadable)*.

Spread the melted caramel over one pretzel, coating all but 2" to 3" at one end. Immediately press popcorn into the caramel. Place on a waxed paper-lined tray and repeat with the remaining pretzels.

Melt the almond bark and drizzle over the pretzels; scatter the decorating sprinkles over the wet bark. **Makes 6**

Festive Popcorn Barque

Ingredients

- 1 (3 oz.) bag kettle corn microwave popcorn
- 1 (12 oz.) pkg. white baking chips
- Food coloring of your choice
- Decorating sprinkles

Pop the popcorn according to package directions and remove unpopped kernels. Set aside ⅓ cup of the baking chips and melt the remainder in a double boiler. Add food coloring and stir until well blended. Spread the melted chips at least ⅛" thick on a waxed paper-lined tray and immediately add the popcorn in an even layer, pressing down gently.

Melt the set-aside chips and drizzle over the popcorn. Scatter the decorating sprinkles over the wet chips. Serves a crowd

To make Homemade Kettle Corn, stir together ½ C. powdered sugar, 2 T. sugar, and 1 tsp. coarse salt. Heat ¼ C. vegetable oil in a big saucepan over medium-high heat; add ¾ C. popcorn kernels and when popping stops, remove the lid and stir in the sugar mixture. You'll need only 6 C. or so to make Festive Popcorn Barque so you'll have plenty of extra kettle corn to munch on. Makes about 18 cups

Peanut Mallow Squares

Ingredients

1 (16.5 oz.) roll refrigerated peanut butter cookie dough

3½ C. mini marshmallows

1 (3 oz.) bag buttered microwave popcorn

1 C. salted peanuts

1 (10 oz.) pkg. peanut butter chips

⅔ C. light corn syrup

¼ C. butter

⅓ C. semi-sweet chocolate chips

⅓ C. milk chocolate chips

Get Started

Preheat the oven to 350°. Coat a 9 x 13" baking pan with cooking spray. With floured fingers, press the cookie dough evenly into the bottom of the pan. Bake for 10 to 12 minutes or until light golden brown. Sprinkle the marshmallows over the crust and bake 3 minutes more until puffed but not brown. Meanwhile, pop the popcorn according to package directions and dump it into a big bowl, removing unpopped kernels; add the peanuts.

Microwave the peanut butter chips with the syrup and butter on high for 1½ minutes or until melted, stirring occasionally. Stir into the popcorn mixture and press evenly over the marshmallows.

Microwave all the chocolate chips together until melted, stirring occasionally, then drizzle over the popcorn layer; cool on a rack for 1 hour. Chill 30 minutes or until set before cutting into bars. **Serves 24**

Honey Cheesecake Tart

Ingredients

- 3 C. unsalted popcorn
- ⅓ C. plus ¼ C. sugar, divided
- 6 T. butter, melted
- 1½ tsp. lemon or orange zest, divided
- 1 (8 oz.) pkg. cream cheese, softened
- 1 (8 oz.) container mascarpone cheese, softened

- 1½ T. honey
- 1 T. cornstarch
- ⅓ C. water
- 1 tsp. lemon or orange juice
- 1 C. fresh raspberries, mashed
- Fresh strawberries & kiwifruit, sliced
- Fresh blackberries

Get Started

Preheat the oven to 350°. Process the popcorn in a blender or food processor 1 cup at a time until finely ground. Mix the ground popcorn, ⅓ cup sugar, butter, and ½ teaspoon zest in a medium bowl until well combined. Press firmly into a foil-lined 9" tart pan. Bake for 10 minutes or until lightly browned; cool completely.

In a medium mixing bowl, beat together the cream cheese, mascarpone cheese, and honey until smooth. Spread filling evenly on prepared crust and chill at least 2 hours.

Before serving, mix cornstarch, water, juice, raspberries, remaining ¼ cup sugar, and remaining 1 teaspoon zest in a saucepan. Bring to a boil over medium heat; boil 1 minute. Cool slightly. Remove tart from pan, spoon raspberry sauce over filling, and top with fresh fruit. Serves 8

Gooey Popcorn Balls

13 C. popcorn   ½ C. butter

45 regular marshmallows

Get Started

Put popcorn in a big bowl. Cut marshmallows in half and place in a heavy saucepan with the butter. Melt over low heat, stirring constantly. Pour marshmallow mixture over the popcorn and stir quickly until well mixed.

With damp hands, quickly form the mixture into balls and set on waxed paper. **Makes 10 to 12**

Stir-ins: To add candy, chop 3 or 4 (2 oz.) candy bars *(we used Snickers, above)* and stir into marshmallow mixture shortly after adding popcorn.

Popcorn balls are delicious on their own, but you can add flair by simply adding extra fun ingredients.

Coat it...

Roll popcorn balls in colorful cereal like Fruity Pebbles *(shown here)*. The sky's the limit, so go ahead and try nonpareils, chopped pistachios or other nuts, toasted coconut, or crushed candies like Smarties. Or get a little crazy and roll them in Pop Rocks candy.

Hide it...

A surprise tucked inside a popcorn ball is a fun treat for all ages. Try Hershey's Kisses *(we used Cherry Cordial, but Caramel, Cookies 'n' Creme, or even plain chocolate would be delicious)*, Rolos, mint patties, bite-size candy bars... you name it. You could even stuff a big colored marshmallow inside!

Pepperoni Little Dippers

Ingredients

2 eggs

½ (8 oz.) tub cream cheese spread

1 T. milk

1½ tsp. Italian seasoning

1 T. grated tomato & basil-flavored
Parmesan cheese

¼ tsp. coarse black pepper

10 C. popcorn

1 C. shredded mozzarella cheese

⅓ C. sliced pepperoni, coarsely chopped

Get Started

Preheat the oven to 350°. Coat an 8 x 8" baking pan with cooking spray; set aside.

In a big bowl, whisk together eggs, cream cheese spread, milk, Italian seasoning, Parmesan cheese, and pepper. Stir in the popcorn, mozzarella cheese, and pepperoni until everything is well coated. Transfer the mixture to the prepared pan, pressing down firmly and evenly.

Bake for 15 minutes or until set and light golden brown. Let stand 5 minutes before cutting. Serve warm with marinara sauce. **Makes 16 pieces**

Kettle Corn M&M Cookies

Ingredients

2 ¾ C. flour

1 ¼ tsp. baking soda

1 tsp. cornstarch

1 tsp. salt

1 C. butter

¾ C. sugar

1 ¼ C. brown sugar

2 tsp. vanilla

2 eggs

1 C. chocolate chips and/or white baking chips

½ C. M&Ms

⅓ C. broken pretzel pieces

2 C. kettle corn

Get Started

Line baking sheets with parchment paper and set aside.

In a big bowl, whisk together the flour, baking soda, cornstarch, and salt; set aside. In a big microwave-safe mixing bowl, microwave butter, until almost melted. Add the sugar, brown sugar, and vanilla and beat on medium speed for 1 minute until smooth and creamy. Add the eggs one at a time, mixing well after each. Reduce speed to low and gradually beat in the flour mixture until a soft dough forms. Fold in the chocolate chips, M&Ms, and pretzel pieces. Lightly stir in the kettle corn. Chill for 2 hours.

Preheat the oven to 350°. Drop dough by large spoonful onto prepared baking sheets, leaving space between cookies. Bake for 11 to 14 minutes, until golden brown around edges. Let cool on the pan for several minutes and then transfer to a cooling rack. **Makes 36**

Ranch

Chile-Lime

Nacho Cheese

24

Ranch

1

Combine 1 T. each onion powder, dried dill, and dried parsley; 1 tsp. each coarse salt and ground black pepper; and ½ tsp. garlic powder. Stir to combine and then sprinkle desired amount over hot buttered popcorn. You can double or triple this recipe if you'd like to have extra on hand for future popcorn cravings. **Makes about ¼ cup**

Chile-Lime

2

Grate the peel of two or three limes to get 2 T. zest and spread out on paper towels to dry. Add the zest to 4 tsp. salt, 2 T. chili powder, 1½ T. ground cumin, 2 tsp. onion powder, and 1 tsp. each garlic powder and cayenne pepper; stir to blend. Shake desired amount over hot buttered popcorn. Put any remaining mixture into a lidded jar for a later popcorn feast. **Makes about ½ cup**

Nacho Cheese

3

Mix ½ C. grated Parmesan cheese; 1 tsp. each paprika, chili powder, and garlic salt; ½ tsp. ground cumin; and ¼ tsp. each cayenne pepper and black pepper. Sprinkle desired amount evenly over hot buttered popcorn. Want even more nacho cheese flavor? Stir nacho-cheese flavored crackers or chips into this mixture, then hold on! **Makes about ⅔ cup**

Apple Chip Caramel Corn

Ingredients

24 C. popcorn

2 (2.5 oz.) bags crisp apple chips

1 C. brown sugar

½ C. butter

1 C. light corn syrup

1 tsp. salt

1 (14 oz.) can sweetened
condensed milk

Get Started

Preheat the oven to 250°. Line a rimmed baking sheet with parchment paper. Dump popcorn into a big bowl. Add apple chips and set aside.

In a heavy saucepan, combine brown sugar, butter, syrup, and salt. Cook over medium heat until it begins to boil, stirring occasionally. Stir in sweetened condensed milk and cook 5 minutes longer, stirring constantly; drizzle over the popcorn mixture and stir until well coated. Spread out evenly on prepared baking sheet and bake for 45 to 50 minutes, stirring every 10 minutes. Break into pieces and cool. **Makes about 25 cups**

Popped Cappuccino Bars

Ingredients

2 C. quick-cooking oats

1 C. Rice Krispies cereal

¼ C. raw coconut chips

¼ C. sliced almonds

¼ tsp. salt

3½ C. popcorn

½ C. almond butter

½ C. honey

2 tsp. instant coffee granules, divided

2½ tsp. vanilla, divided

2 T. butter

12 vanilla candy melts

¼ tsp. shortening

1¼ C. dark chocolate chips, divided

Coarse salt, optional

Get Started

Line an 8 x 8" baking pan with waxed paper. In a big bowl, stir together the oats, cereal, coconut, almonds, and salt. Put the popcorn into a separate bowl. Set all aside.

Melt together the almond butter and honey. Add 1½ teaspoons coffee granules; stir to dissolve. Stir in 1½ teaspoons vanilla and mix into the set-aside oats mixture. Press mixture firmly into the prepared pan; freeze the crust for 30 minutes. Melt together the butter, candy melts, and shortening. Stir in the remaining ½ teaspoon coffee granules to dissolve; stir in the remaining 1 teaspoon vanilla and mix into the popcorn.

Melt ¾ cup chocolate chips and spread over the chilled crust. Press the popcorn mixture into the wet chocolate. Melt the remaining ½ cup chocolate chips and drizzle over the popcorn; sprinkle with coarse salt. Chill to harden; cut into bars. **Serves 8**

Extreme PB Chow

Place 9 C. popcorn in a big bowl with 1 C. mini Reese's Peanut Butter Cups. Melt together 1 C. milk chocolate chips, ½ C. creamy peanut butter, and ¼ C. butter; stir until smooth. Stir in 1 tsp. vanilla and pour mixture over popcorn; mix until evenly coated. Stir in 1½ C. powdered sugar until all pieces are coated. **Makes 10 cups**

Carrot Cake Buddies

Melt together 1 C. white candy melts and ½ C. purchased cream cheese frosting. Stir in 1 tsp. vanilla and pour over a mixture of 9 C. popcorn and 1 C. chopped pecans; mix until well coated. Stir together ¾ C. dry carrot cake mix and ½ C. powdered sugar; add to the popcorn and stir to coat. Dump out onto waxed paper. Melt ½ C. Caramel Bits and drizzle over the top, if you'd like. **Makes 10 cups**

Simply PB Munch

Pop 1 (3 oz.) bag buttered microwave popcorn; remove unpopped kernels. Dump popcorn into a big bowl with 1 C. small pretzels and 1 C. salted peanuts. Melt together ¼ C. creamy peanut butter and 2 T. butter; stir until smooth. Let the hot mixture set for a few minutes to cool slightly and then drizzle over the popcorn mixture; stir to coat. Sprinkle 1 C. powdered sugar over the top and toss until coated. **Makes 8 cups**

Cinnamon Waffle Mix

Place 2 C. Rice Chex cereal, 2 C. Waffle Crisp cereal, and 7 C. popcorn in a big bowl. Melt together ¾ C. white baking chips and ¾ C. cinnamon baking chips, stirring until smooth and blended; pour over the popcorn mixture and stir until coated. Let stand 5 minutes, then stir in 1 C. powdered sugar. Stir in some extra Waffle Crisp, if desired. **Makes 11 cups**

Cheesy-Pop Cornbread

Ingredients

4 C. popcorn

1 C. yellow cornmeal

2 T. sugar

2 tsp. baking powder

½ tsp. salt

1 egg

1 C. milk

¼ C. vegetable oil

1 C. shredded Pepper Jack cheese

1 (4.25 oz.) can diced green chiles, drained

Get Started

Preheat the oven to 400°. Coat an 8 x 8" baking dish with cooking spray and set aside.

Process the popcorn in a blender or food processor until finely ground. Pour into a large bowl and add the cornmeal, sugar, baking powder, and salt; stir until combined.

In a small bowl, beat together the egg, milk, and oil; add to cornmeal mixture and stir until just blended. Scatter the cheese and chiles over the batter and stir lightly. Pour batter into prepared pan and bake for 25 minutes or until cornbread tests done with a toothpick. Cut into small squares and serve with sour cream and bell pepper relish, salsa, or jalapeño jelly. **Makes 16 pieces**

Bacon Caramel Corn

Ingredients

8 bacon strips

2 T. vegetable oil

¾ C. popcorn kernels

1 C. butter

2 C. brown sugar

½ C. light corn syrup

½ tsp. salt

½ tsp. baking soda

1½ tsp. vanilla

Get Started

Preheat the oven to 250°. Line two rimmed baking sheets with parchment paper; set aside.

Cut bacon into small pieces and cook until crisp. Remove bacon to paper towels and pour 1 T. of the bacon drippings into a large stock pot with the oil. Set over medium heat and add popcorn kernels; cover. When popping begins, remove from the heat for 1 minute, then return to the heat and shake until all kernels have popped. Transfer the popcorn to a big bowl, remove unpopped kernels, and stir in the bacon.

Melt the butter in a heavy saucepan. Stir in the brown sugar, syrup, and salt; bring to a boil, stirring constantly. Let the mixture boil undisturbed for 4 minutes. Remove from the heat and stir in baking soda and vanilla *(it will be foamy)*; pour over the popcorn, stirring to coat. Transfer to prepared baking sheets and bake for 1 hour, stirring every 15 minutes. Break into pieces and cool. **Makes about 18 cups**

Popcorn Puffs

Ingredients

¾ C. flour

2 T. sugar

¾ tsp. baking powder

¼ tsp. baking soda

⅛ tsp. salt

1 egg

½ C. milk

½ tsp. vanilla

6 C. buttered
  microwave popcorn

5 to 6 C. canola oil

Powdered sugar & coarse salt

Stir together the flour, sugar, baking powder, baking soda, and salt in a medium bowl. In another bowl, whisk together the egg, milk, and vanilla until blended; add to flour mixture, whisking well *(batter will be fairly thin)*.

Heat 3" of oil to 400° in a heavy saucepan or deep-fryer. Working in batches, drop some of the popcorn into the batter, stirring to coat. Fry popcorn pieces in hot oil until golden brown on each side. Drain on paper towels and immediately sprinkle with powdered sugar, salt, or both. Delicious on their own or dipped in syrup, cheese sauce, or honey-mustard. **Serves 6**

Ice Cream Popwiches

Ingredients

- 3 T. butter
- 3 C. mini marshmallows
- 6 C. caramel corn
- 1 C. salted peanuts
- 3 to 4 C. vanilla ice cream
- Mini chocolate chips or chopped M&Ms

Line a baking sheet with parchment paper and coat with cooking spray; set aside.

Melt butter in a big saucepan over medium-low heat. Add marshmallows and stir until melted. Remove from the heat and stir in caramel corn and peanuts; cool slightly.

With damp hands, shape about ⅓ cup of the popcorn mixture into a ball. Set on the prepared pan and flatten to form a cookie shape. Repeat with remaining popcorn mixture. Freeze about 20 minutes to set.

Put a scoop of ice cream *(⅓ to ½ cup)* between two cookies and press together lightly. Roll edges in chocolate chips or M&Ms to cover the ice cream. Freeze until the ice cream is firm. Wrap individually in plastic wrap for longer storage.
Makes about 8

Candy
Almond Truffles

Ingredients

- 4 C. popcorn
- 3 (1.76 oz.) Snickers Almond candy bars, cut into smaller pieces
- ½ tsp. coarse salt
- ½ C. each milk chocolate & semi-sweet chocolate chips
- 1 T. shortening

Get Started

Line a tray with waxed paper. Place the popcorn in a big bowl. Set aside.

Heat the candy bars in the microwave until melted, and immediately pour over the popcorn; sprinkle with salt and stir until well blended. Roll into balls about 1½" in diameter and set them on the prepared tray.

Melt all the chocolate chips together with the shortening in a double boiler over medium-low heat, stirring constantly. Reduce the heat to low.

One at a time, poke a skewer into the popcorn balls and hold above the double boiler. Drizzle with chocolate until coated; set them on the prepared tray.

Refrigerate about 30 minutes or until the chocolate has set.

Makes about 15

Poppin' Blueberry Muffins

Ingredients

½ tsp. cinnamon

2 T. plus ¼ C. sugar, divided

5 C. popcorn

1½ C. flour

1 T. baking powder

½ tsp. salt

½ C. dried blueberries

1 C. milk

1 egg

2 T. vegetable oil

½ tsp. almond extract

¼ C. sliced almonds

Get Started

Preheat the oven to 400°. Line 12 standard muffin cups with paper liners *(or coat with cooking spray)*. In a small bowl, stir together the cinnamon and 2 tablespoons sugar; set aside.

Process the popcorn in a blender or food processor until finely ground. Pour into a big bowl and add flour, baking powder, salt, blueberries, and the remaining ¼ cup sugar; stir to combine.

In a small bowl, whisk together the milk, egg, oil, and almond extract. Pour over flour mixture and stir until just combined. Spoon the batter into prepared muffin cups, filling each about half full. Sprinkle with almonds and set-aside cinnamon-sugar mixture. Bake 15 to 18 minutes or until tops are lightly browned. Makes 12

Red Hot

Preheat the oven to 250°. Line a rimmed baking sheet with parchment paper. Dump 5 C. popcorn into a big bowl. In a small saucepan over medium heat, combine ¼ C. water and ½ C. red hot candies. Cook until melted, stirring often; drizzle over the popcorn and stir to combine. Transfer to prepared baking sheet and bake for 20 minutes, stirring halfway through baking time.
Makes 5 cups

Lucky Mix

Pour 4 C. Lucky Charms cereal and 6 C. popcorn into a big bowl. Melt 1½ C. white baking chips and pour over the cereal mixture; toss to coat. Spread mixture in a single layer on a waxed paper-lined tray and immediately toss on extra marshmallows from the cereal box, if you'd like. Let stand until set. Makes 10 cups

Orange Dreamsicle

Put 14 C. popcorn in a big bowl. Zest and juice 1 orange; set the zest aside and transfer ⅓ C. of the juice to a microwave-safe bowl *(discard any remaining juice)*. Add ½ tsp. orange flavoring *(or more to taste)* and 1 (12 oz.) pkg. white baking chips to the juice and microwave until melted, stirring until smooth. Pour the mixture over the popcorn and stir until well coated; dump out onto waxed paper and immediately sprinkle with the set-aside zest. Let stand until the coating is set.
Makes 14 cups

PBJ

Put 4 C. popcorn in each of two bowls. Melt together ½ C. white candy melts and 1 T. peanut butter; stir until smooth and pour over the popcorn in one bowl. Mix well and spread out on parchment paper to cool. Melt ½ C. white candy melts with 1½ T. grape jelly; stir until smooth and pour over the popcorn in the other bowl. Mix well and spread out on parchment paper. Once cool, stir the two flavors together.
Makes 8 cups

Cranberry Popcorn Biscotti

Ingredients

3 eggs

½ tsp. vanilla

2 C. flour, plus more
for shaping

1 C. sugar

1 tsp. baking soda

⅛ tsp. salt

3 C. popcorn

½ C. chopped dried
cranberries, cherries,
or apricots

White and/or chocolate
almond bark

Get Started

Preheat the oven to 300°. Coat two baking sheets with
cooking spray; set aside.

Beat eggs and vanilla in a big bowl. Sift together 2 cups flour,
sugar, baking soda, and salt; add to egg, mixing thoroughly.
Stir in popcorn and cranberries *(dough will be sticky)*.

Cover a work surface with a little flour and turn dough out
onto flour; divide into three equal pieces. Roll each piece
into a log about 8" long and 2" wide, adding flour as needed
to prevent sticking. Transfer logs to the prepared baking
sheets, leaving plenty of room between them.

Bake for 30 minutes; remove from the oven *(but don't turn
off oven)*. Let cool 5 minutes. Transfer to a cutting board and
cut into ¾" diagonal slices. Arrange slices on baking sheets;
bake 20 minutes longer, flipping them over after 10 minutes.

Remove cookies to cooling racks set over waxed paper.
Drizzle with melted almond bark. Makes about 35

Melt-in-Your-Mouth Popcorn Fudge

Ingredients

½ C. butter, cubed

¾ C. sour cream

2 C. sugar

1 tsp. salt

1 (12 oz.) pkg. white
    baking chips

1 (7 oz.) container
    marshmallow crème

1 tsp. clear vanilla

½ tsp. butter flavoring

3 C. caramel corn or kettle
    corn, divided

Get Started

Line a 9 x 9" pan with foil and coat with cooking spray;
set aside.

Heat the butter in a big saucepan over low heat until nearly
melted, stirring occasionally. Increase the heat to medium.
Add the sour cream, sugar, and salt, stirring until the sugar
dissolves. Cook until the mixture comes to a boil; attach a
candy thermometer and cook until temperature reaches 235°.

Remove the pan from the heat and quickly add baking chips
and marshmallow crème, stirring vigorously until melted.
Stir in vanilla and butter flavoring. Then stir in 2 cups of the
caramel corn until well blended.

Pour the mixture into the prepared pan, smoothing it evenly.
Scatter the remaining 1 cup caramel corn over the top,
pressing down lightly.

Let stand several hours to set before cutting into 1" squares.
Makes 81 pieces

Popcorn Haystacks

Ingredients

1 (3 oz.) bag buttered
  microwave popcorn

2 C. chow mein noodles

½ C. white baking chips

¾ C. butterscotch chips

¾ C. peanut butter chips

Pop popcorn according to package directions; remove unpopped kernels and transfer popcorn to a big bowl. Dump in the chow mein noodles.

Melt together the white baking chips, butterscotch chips, and peanut butter chips; stir until smooth. Pour melted mixture over the popcorn mixture and stir until evenly coated. Drop heaping tablespoons of the mixture onto waxed paper-lined baking sheets. Chill for 1 to 2 hours or until firm. **Makes 24**

Strawberry Shortbread

Ingredients

- 2 C. flour
- ½ C. powdered sugar
- 1 C. butter, cubed
- 1 egg white, lightly beaten
- 1 (12 oz.) jar strawberry preserves
- 4 C. popcorn
- ¼ C. dark chocolate chips

Preheat the oven to 350°. Grease a 9 x 13" pan; set aside.

In a food processor, process flour and powdered sugar; add butter and process until butter pieces are pea-size. Press evenly into the prepared pan. Brush egg white over the crust. Bake for 25 minutes or until golden brown.

Remove from the oven and immediately spread preserves over the crust. Press popcorn into the preserves and set aside to cool.

Melt the chocolate chips and drizzle over the popcorn layer. Set aside until the chocolate has cooled before cutting into bars. **Serves 18**

Tangy Molasses Corn

Ingredients

6 C. popcorn

½ tsp. baking soda

⅛ tsp. ground nutmeg

2 tsp. vanilla

½ tsp. each almond
   extract, butter flavoring
   & rum flavoring

¼ C. butter

½ C. sugar

1½ T. molasses

½ T. water

¼ tsp. coarse salt

Get Started

Preheat the oven to 200°. Put the popcorn in a big bowl. Line a rimmed baking sheet with parchment paper. Put the baking soda and nutmeg in a small bowl. In a separate small bowl, combine the vanilla, almond extract, butter flavoring, and rum flavoring. Set all aside.

Attach a candy thermometer to a heavy saucepan. Put the butter, sugar, molasses, water, and salt in the saucepan and cook over medium heat until the temperature reaches 305°, stirring occasionally. Carefully stir in the extract mixture and then the baking soda mixture *(it will get foamy)*. Pour the hot mixture over the popcorn and stir to coat thoroughly. Spread onto the prepared baking sheet and bake for 1 hour. When cool, break the popcorn into pieces. **Makes 6 cups**

To make Tangy Molasses Corn Cones, layer Nutella, cashews, banana slices, Tangy Molasses Corn, and your favorite yogurt in ice cream cones.

Loaded Granola Bars

Ingredients

½ C. whole natural almonds

1 (2.25 oz.) pkg. pumpkin seeds

8 C. popcorn

1½ C. old-fashioned oats

1 (3.5 oz.) pkg. dried blueberries

⅔ C. honey

⅔ C. brown sugar

2 T. butter

Get Started

Line a 9 x 13" pan with foil; coat with cooking spray and set aside.

Put almonds and pumpkin seeds in a dry skillet. Toast over medium heat for 10 minutes or until golden brown; dump into a big bowl with the popcorn, oats, and blueberries.

Combine honey, brown sugar, and butter in a small saucepan; bring to a boil over low heat and boil for 2 minutes. Pour hot mixture over popcorn mixture and stir until well coated.

Transfer the mixture to the prepared pan and use damp hands to press firmly into an even layer. Chill for 2 hours before cutting into bars. **Serves 18**

Caramel Corn Candy

Line a baking sheet with waxed paper. Melt 1 (20 oz.) pkg. chocolate almond bark according to package directions; stir until smooth. Pour the chocolate onto the prepared baking sheet and spread to ¼" thickness. While it's still wet, evenly scatter 1 C. each caramel corn, salted peanuts, chocolate-covered raisins, and broken pretzels over the top; press gently. Refrigerate until firm. Remove foil and break into pieces. **Serves a crowd**

Peppermint Poppers

Line a rimmed baking sheet with parchment paper. Put 16 C. popcorn in a big bowl. Melt 1 C. mint baking chips and pour over the popcorn; toss to coat. Spread the popcorn out onto the prepared baking sheet and immediately scatter decorating sprinkles over the top. Melt 2 squares chocolate almond bark and drizzle over the popcorn. Refrigerate until set and then break into pieces. Makes 16 cups

Peanut Butter Grahams

Line a rimmed baking sheet with waxed paper. In a big bowl, toss together 4 C. each popcorn, salted peanuts, and Golden Grahams cereal. Melt together ⅔ C. creamy peanut butter and ½ C. honey; drizzle over the popcorn mixture, stirring to coat well. Spread onto the prepared baking sheet. Melt ½ C. white baking chips and drizzle over the popcorn mixture; do the same with ½ C. semi-sweet chocolate chips. Chill to set and break into pieces. **Makes 12 cups**

M&M Magic

Line a rimmed baking sheet with waxed paper. Dump 12 C. buttered popcorn into a big bowl. Melt 1 (20 oz.) pkg. white almond bark according to package directions, pour over the popcorn, and stir to combine. Spread mixture out onto the prepared baking sheet. Toss on some decorating sprinkles and M&Ms, pressing gently into the popcorn. Let stand until set and then break into pieces. Makes 12 cups

55

Popcorn Salsa Bites

Ingredients

Plain popcorn

1 C. cooked brown rice, cooled

1 C. shredded Pepper Jack cheese

4 eggs

1 (16 oz.) jar thick salsa, plus more
  for serving

½ C. sour cream, plus more for serving

½ tsp. each salt & black pepper

¾ C. crushed corn chips

Get Started

Preheat the oven to 350°. Coat 48 mini muffin cups with
cooking spray. Set aside.

Crush enough popcorn to make 2 cups and dump in a
medium bowl; add rice and cheese. In a large bowl, beat eggs
well. Stir in 2 cups salsa, ½ cup sour cream, salt, and pepper.
Add popcorn mixture and stir well. Divide mixture evenly
among prepared muffin cups, filling nearly full. Sprinkle chips
and/or some uncrushed popcorn over filling, pressing down
lightly. Bake for 15 to 20 minutes or until lightly browned.
Serve warm with more salsa and sour cream. Makes 48

Caramel Corn Oatmeal Cookies

Ingredients

Caramel corn

¾ C. sugar, divided

½ C. butter, softened

1 egg

½ tsp. almond extract

¾ C. flour

½ tsp. baking powder

½ tsp. baking soda

½ C. quick-cooking oats

Get Started

Preheat the oven to 350°. Line two baking sheets with parchment paper. Lightly crush caramel corn to measure ½ cup. Put ¼ cup sugar in a bowl. Set all aside.

In a mixing bowl, beat butter and remaining ½ cup sugar until light and fluffy; add egg and beat until well mixed. Stir in the set-aside crushed caramel corn, almond extract, flour, baking powder, baking soda, oats, and ¾ cup uncrushed caramel corn.

Roll heaping tablespoons of dough into balls and roll in set-aside sugar to coat. Arrange on prepared baking sheets and bake for 12 minutes or until golden brown. Let stand 2 minutes before removing to a cooling rack. Makes 24

Kale Chip Parmesan Corn

Ingredients

5 or 6 kale leaves

3½ T. olive oil, divided

1 tsp. chili powder

¼ tsp. garlic powder

½ tsp. salt

⅔ C. popcorn kernels

3 T. melted butter

6 T. grated Parmesan cheese

1 tsp. dried parsley

Preheat the oven to 350°. Line two rimmed baking sheets with foil. Remove and discard the stems from the kale leaves, tear the leaves into bite-size pieces, and put them in a big bowl; drizzle with 2 tablespoons oil and toss to coat.

Stir together the chili powder, garlic powder, and salt; sprinkle over the kale and toss to coat. Spread the kale in a single layer on the prepared baking sheets. Bake for 12 to 15 minutes or until crispy but still green.

Heat the remaining 1½ tablespoons oil in a large saucepan, add the popcorn kernels, and shake the pan over medium heat until the popping nearly stops. Remove the pan from the heat until the popping stops completely. Drizzle popcorn with melted butter and stir in the cheese and parsley. Combine the popcorn and the kale; stir gently. **Makes about 15 cups**

Fudgy Butterscotch Bars

Ingredients

- 1 (12 oz.) pkg. semi-sweet chocolate chips
- 2 T. shortening
- 12 C. popcorn
- 3 T. butter
- 4 C. mini marshmallows
- 1 C. butterscotch chips

Line a 9 x 9" pan with foil and grease the foil; set aside. Melt chocolate chips with shortening, stirring until smooth; chill for 15 minutes or until thickened.

Meanwhile, put the popcorn in a big bowl. Melt the butter in a heavy saucepan over low heat. Stir in the marshmallows and butterscotch chips until melted and smooth. Stir the marshmallow mixture into the popcorn until well coated. With greased hands, press half the mixture firmly into the prepared pan; spread the chilled chocolate mixture evenly over the popcorn and press the remaining popcorn mixture firmly over the chocolate. Chill for 30 minutes.

Remove foil and cut into bars. **Serves 20**

Candied Corn

Ingredients

Butter for greasing

11 C. popcorn

1 (14 oz.) can sweetened
condensed milk

1 (3 oz.) pkg. gelatin,
any flavor

Get Started

Preheat the oven to 300°. Line a work surface with a big sheet of foil. Line two rimmed baking sheets with foil, extending it over all sides; grease all the foil with butter. Divide the popcorn among the baking sheets and put them in the oven to warm.

In a medium saucepan, combine the sweetened condensed milk and dry gelatin; heat over low heat about 5 minutes or until slightly thickened, stirring constantly. Drizzle the mixture evenly over the warm popcorn; stir to coat. Spread out evenly on prepared baking sheets. Bake for 20 minutes, stirring every 5 minutes.* Carefully transfer the popcorn to the prepared work surface. Cool and then break into pieces.
Makes 11 cups.

* If both baking sheets can't fit side by side in your oven, bake one at a time. Then watch closely – if the popcorn begins to brown, move the baking sheet to a different oven rack, either higher or lower, depending on your oven. (We made three batches – lime, wild strawberry, and berry blue.)

Index